THE LOST BOOK OF ETERNITY

SUMIT BISWAS

Contents

Contents

Contents

Preface

"A poem is not just a page with words
It's not just a collection of beautiful words
It's just a way to convey
The truth to the reality
Through the bond of these words."

"*THE LOST BOOK OF ETERNITY*" is a collection of poetry on various topics. some dealing with a particular kind of emotion, some about life and some about love, stories with a touch of scariness in it. The book is a wholesome experience of various feelings with happiness filled in every page. Hope that you will have a great experience by reading the thoughts coming from a young writer's mind in the form of beautiful words displayed on every page.

1. I wrote a song for you

I wrote a song for you
for the person you were
for the person you grew into
for everything you did,
for the things you still do
i wrote a song for you...
for the people you found
for the people who lost you
for the moments of misery,
for the times you fought through
i wrote a song for you...
for the friends you always dreamed of
for the real ones and the true
for the love you always give,
i wrote a song for you.

2. Patience & Self Control

Life is the race where birth is the start,
The nourishment of the soul
is done by purity of the heart
The impact of yours depends
on the words you speak,
Some toxic & negative thoughts
can make your mind weak.
The true form of devotion helps
in liberation of the soul,
Patience & self control helps you
to focus on your goal...
You are limited by your thoughts
so keep them wide
So that your mind thinks free
without being tired.....

3. Heart- It's a temple

Stop giving your heart out
Like It's a renting space
It's a temple
The fun happens outside of the premises
And the dirt shouldn't get it in
Start Respecting your heart
and for once treat it like your own
No one would take care of it
like you yourself could do
So remember only one gets into the heart
& rest the garbage including slippers
should stay outside......

4. Once upon a time...

Some say I'm mad,
Some say I'm confused.
My mind is a bomb,
My thoughts are diffused.
When i said, stay calm,
My heart refused.
I am not very happy
Does that mean, I'm abused?
No scar on my body,
But my heart is very bruised.
Whenever something happens,
My past is always accused,
But when i feel pain,
Then why my heart is amused?
It's shattered into pieces,
where once love was infused.
You did it on purpose,
I know.....
But you are excused.

5. Forever Friendship

Sometimes in life, you find a special friend.
Someone who changes your life just by being part of it.
Someone who makes you laugh until you can't stop.
Someone who makes you believe that
there really is good in the world.
Someone who convinces you
that there really is an unlocked door
just waiting for you to open it
This is forever friendship.
When you're down and the world seems dark
and empty your forever friend lifts you up in spirit
and makes that dark and empty world
suddenly seem bright and full.
Your forever friend gets you through the hard times,
the sad times and the confused times.
If you turn and walk away your forever friend follows.
If you lose your way,
your forever friend guides you and cheers you on.
Your forever friend hold your hand and
tells you that everything is going to be okay.
And if you find such a friend,
you feel happy and complete

because you need not worry
You have a forever friend,
and forever has no end".

• 6 •

6. One person is enough for beautiful life...

You are the person who wipes my tears
but you will be the person
who makes me cry
You are the person
who fights with me
but you will be the person
who fights for me
You are the person
who celebrates my victory
but you will be the person
who consoles me in my failures
You are the person who teases me
but you will be the person
who fights with the person who teased me
when I was a child
You hold my hand as a stranger
but now without you I'll be nothing.

7. Never give up

This journey is yours
There will be peace,
there will be chaos.
Somedays you will pour love from your soul....
Somedays you will struggle to feel whole.
There will be days
when you giggle like a child...
There will be days
where nobody has a clue you cried.
Somedays will be easy,
Somedays the fight will get tough.
The downs are meant to come
but there will be ups.
That's why you need to get going
and never give up.

8. I'm searching for you...

I'm searching for you,
Where have you been.
Please be fast,
My heart is so keen.
You are my only support,
When whole world is mean.
You have been real good to me,
Cause your heart is clean.
Love in your eyes,
Is what i have seen.
There will be no one in between.
If you want to imagine,
Imagine it to be a movie scene.
I will be your king,
And you will be the queen.

9. Just stay kind

I don't need you
To type a paragraph
One word from you
Is treated like an autograph
When my phone beeps
I miss my sleeps
Is it an easy identification?
Oh My.......
I am always waiting for
a notification
It's that one simple effort
That gives a clear report
I know that you are fine
But I saw a bottle of wine
It is not easy to read your mind
But just stay kind.

10. Everyone needs someone

Everybody needs somebody,
when they are tired of being bold,
when there are secrets to be told,
when they want someone to hold,
when there is joy of great worth to share, when no one else seems
to care,
when they're alone and
their soul feels bare,
Everyone needs someone
who will be there.

11. A love that never ends

I may not say
But what I feel for you
Is more than
All the words that may mean
I may not show
But what you mean to me
Is beyond
What this world may seem
We may never meet !!!
But I will always wait for you
In a place...
That no one knows or has seen.

12. Moon & Me

From the entire exhausting day
To the confection and melody night
The rhythm of cold breezes,
Make my ears adored,
Thinking of a person who can Handel my tone,
Not only aggression
but the love Behind that,
Moon starts to smile,
Said hey,! Mr.
don't expect as you are doing in a while
In the era of fakeness,
Try to keep yourself happy on your own,
Not wait for that someone can make
a stage for you full of red carpets,
Because they are dangerous Thorns,
I start revealing my secrets to the moon,
He uncommunicative listens to me
without making any joke,
I shed my tear while conveying my unknown,
He said don't cry,
I daily see many peoples
who make warm-heart broke,

I am always for you
Share your view
I will not tell that, Even to the stars,
I am solely yours,
Just parcel your views and vanished
from the unforgettable thoughts !!!

13. Everything is temporary : Except yourself

No matter how bad your day is
but your life is not bad,
every situation happens for the reason
and that reason will not acceptable
at the beginning,
but in the end you will get your fruit!
Stop expecting things from others
I know you are the best,
strong and beautiful person
you don't need someone
who always tells you this stuff,
all you need is to believe in yourself.
You are a goal-directed soul
and with millstone's powerful thoughts
you are best the way you are.
Never change yourself for someone
because no one gonna stay for long
and make you happy in this world
expect yourself.
So, "BE POSITIVE AND JUST SMILE.

14. Everyone is wearing a mask ?

I am ready to fall.
I am ready to cross
every hurdle big or small.
But I don't need people anymore.
For supporting me or
for counting my score.
Because they aren't constant.
So their presence in my life
is almost insignificant.
I am my own cheerleader.
My support system and
my only persuader.
With me my parents are always there
But except them noone is playing fair.
Everyone is just wearing a mask.
They behave as if they are
performing some task.
Of pleasing everyone around them.
This has become a standard system.
I wish people realise the

importance of bing real.
And feel care and love
without any fake layer.

• 17 •

15. People are mortal, love is not.

we vow forevers,
but how many of us really mean it?
we only pick out the beautiful flowers from
the garden and make ourselves love them.
But true love lies in picking up the withered ones and
putting together them love their own self first.......
The ones who fell for hearts
didn't care about the faces.
and the ones who fell for faces
did not care about their own heart.....
Love does not come with conditions,
love is a condition.......
people define love as
care, compatibility, sacrifice, compromises, and so on.
But when we go and
define something, we restrict its growth.
and love doesn't, rather it shouldn't have boundaries,
it was never meant to be constrained.

16. Life is precious

Life is precious because
it's a one time thing
there's no pause, rewind, or fast forward button......
It doesn't matter
if you don't know what you're going to do tomorrow
because that's also what makes life exciting —
we are the authors of our stories
so take everything in,
do what you want, do it all,
and smile more because
you deserve to be happy.

17. Everything will be okay in the end.

Have you ever been in a phase of your life..
Where nothing is wrong..
But also nothing is right...
Where you can't be happy
But also there is no reason to be sad....
Where everything seems to be falling apart...
But also everything standing still.....
If you are in this phase....
I want to tell you that
You are not alone...
We all are figuring things out
And we will figure this out too....
So the only thing which we can do is
Try to be happy and
just trust the process..
And remember.....
Everything will be okay in the end.
If it is not okay, it's not the end.

18. Difference between : Judgement and Understanding.

They are many beautiful things in you,
might not be visible to everyone
unless someone try to know you deeply....
Unless someone's intention
is to only understand you
rather than judging you....
Some might think you are cold hearted
Some might think you are self contained...
Some might think you are unemotional.
Only the person who knows you for good
understands your silence has thousands of emotion,
well of feelings,
unexplainable love and care.

19. Dreams

Close your eyes Imagine that all of
your dreams have come true,
You're living your dream life
Doing the things you want
Surrounded by the people you want...
How does it feel? Amazing !! right?
Now open your eyes and get to work!
Don't waste time simply dreaming about your dreams......
Instead, make actual plans on how to reach them...
You don't have to run or make big steps every day...
don't pressure yourself to that extent...
Even baby steps count as progress...
So appreciate those too...
There's no time for disappointments and giving up...
that time cannot be Wasted...
Another day, another opportunity to
become better, stronger and happier.

20. You Deserve the Best

Those who belong to you
will never run away,
only run towards you.
It's right when you're both at ease
with each other and everything
just simply flows.
If you're in need of putting in more effort
than another consistently then perhaps it's time to let that bridge
burn.
You have so much love to give,
if they are unwilling to appreciate it,
then they're undeserving of you.
There will be someone
who will give you the same effort in return,
it just may not be them and that's okay.....
Allow yourself to be respected.
Allow yourself to be loved the way you deserve to be.....
Please do not chase a heart that is cold and closed off,
you're worth so much.
I hope you remember that.
Also, please never change the way you love.
You were never the reason they would run away,

it was always something deep within themselves....
It was never you. Be kind to yourself and never change.
The right one will love every inch of you
including the way you love others.......
And Remember You Are Good Enough and also
You Deserve the Best.

21. Nothing is guaranteed

What you've today,
might be gone tomorrow.
What is missing today,
will knock at your door tomorrow.
Therefore, at each stage of your life,
there's something that's
getting added and subtracted too....
Be grateful for what you've now, As it may be gone tomorrow,
Be grateful for what's coming
As it may be something
you've been waiting for from a long time.....
Be grateful , Embrace each stage of your life gracefully.

22. Everything happens for a reason....

The real magic happens
when you accept life, All of it.
The new, the old, the hard times and the good.
We aren't here to be happy every day,
we are here to feel all the emotions.
We aren't here to stand still,
we are here to change, evolve and move.
Sometimes the new will be welcomed,
other times it will be hard.
But please know that
life is to be an adventure, an experience.
Life is the everyday mundane moments.
Life is the journey.
And life is accepting that whatever happens,
everything that happens, is beautiful,
all in its own way.

23. Fixed mindset

Many people have fixed mindset
And if you don't fit in it
They think negative about you
And start behaving accordingly
And then name and tag you
For being negative
But the fact is
There is nothing wrong with you
It is all about them And their thoughts. ?

24. You're not alone....

You're not alone....
This entire universe is with you
O my friend, bear a little patience.....
Angels are there too.
The darkness can't dim your light....
You're a beautiful fireflie
I know it's paining.....
But you're more than your pain
Remember !!!
Nothing can shatter your way.....
Be patient and trust in the process !!

25. I'll Wait For You!!

I can't promise you moon & stars,

But all i can give you is my heart,

Maybe my verse would be enough,

To love you underneath this stars,

So tell me please my beloved,i

Would it be enough for you,

Or i have to fight the gods,

i will patiently wait for you,

As i dream about spending eternity,

in your arms till heavens fall.

26. Finding Someone

I don't want a love
With whom i can grow old...
My soul is tried of the future
Which is yet unexplored...
My heart seeks a love
Which is alive & well today.....
I don't know what tomorrow holds
So in this moment of time...
I need to find Someone
Who can be my home someday.

27. I am your greatest fan

I want someone with whom,
I can share my joy, pain & sorrows
and such people are really few.
That's why there are best friends,
And I got a perfect friend like you.
You multiply my happiness in my joy,
You heal my broken soul when I am sad,
Whether it's a bright morning or a dark night,
You're always there for me no matter if I am wrong or right,
When I am with you, I can be true & real Forgetting all the
discipline, etiquette & the fake life.
Some moments spent with you are the best & ideal,
Everything is sweet with you whether it's a fight, argument or a
strife,
So this words are for telling you,
That's how thankful I am.
You're the best person in this world,
And dear I am your greatest fan.

28. 'I missed you today but that's nothing new'

'I missed you today but that's nothing new,
I missed you a million times yesterday too,
I picked up my phone to talk with you,
Then i realised again i can't text it to you

I saw your bright smile at least twenty times
And then I remember it's all my mind
I drive without presence the world feel surreal,
And on comes your song and his doesn't seems real,

I missed you today 'l missed you tomorrow
There seems to be no coming end to this sorrow.

29. I got lost in this life

I could never hate her
No matter what I tried
My heart didn't allowed me
Even today after all this while
People said a lot of things
About her in my ears
So I left them all behind....
For me she was a gift of life
Maybe because I loved her
Without any expectations
That's why whenever Her memories flash by
A smile arrives on my face
A dream that remain a dream
As I got lost in this life.

30. I will wait for you...

I will wait for you
let the world say
Whatever it has to
It doesn't matter
If I have to wait
An eternity for you
I will be standing there
Where you left me
A place between Heaven & hell
Beyond hope & faith
I hope to see you again
Now I am going to sleep
I will see you in my dreams.

31. Life is beautiful and kind

Life is beautiful and kind
if we leave what's past behind,
But we don't and be unkind to our everything,
our body, soul and mind
We keep on playing the same tape again and rewind again,
Feeling tension with the present
causing an unimaginable strain,
There by learning to let go by keeping memories on roll,
Imagining future scenarios with a lost sense of forlorn,
So we do hope that last moments never happen or last forever,
But the truth is last moments never end,
those are the ones we sure will remember.

32. Father

Your hair is turning white, from grey,
Your face is getting wrinkles day by day,
You seem tired with some physical issues,
How can I accept you're this weaker version father?

You walk slowly, when I rush to catch something,
Your move carefully with all the precautions,
Your voice is cracked and sometimes sounds strange,
How can I accept you're this weaker version father?
I had learned walking by holding your finger,
You gave me confidence in how to make the balance,
It's you, who told me how to pronounce words,
How can I accept you're this weaker version father?
My way is tough and hard, I still have rocks to cross,
I still fight with the phobia of heights and depth,
You're still my Superhero to guide me, in every step,
How can I accept you're this weaker version father?
I beg my Almighty in my prayer,
Please be kind to me and be fairer,
I'm desirous to stay along with my father here,
How can I accept you're this weaker version father?

33. Who Am I ?

What would I be If I didn't write any poem
What would I have become?
The present It haunts me, I'm scared
The future is ingrained me and the past hurts so bad.

If I question I'm lost don't know where to start
Cause each day feels like a dart'
Aiming constantly towards something
Which I don't want?, I'm fermenting.

I'm emersed in doubt as I try to defend my thought
But it provokes the meaning of the life I sought
Raises a question of who I am ? I feel confined
Cause my own credence is inherent, I'm bind.

I try to break free and seek the truth I grieve
But deeper my reality anchors me, will i be able to leave
To figure out who I am beneath the shadow they describe
But to do that the reason for life is what I must bribe.

34. Home

Home is the place, a territory,
Where we find our comfort,
We love to stay and to live and grow,
We like to return and never let it go.

Home is the place, a territory ,
Our internal weakness to hold,
A powerful zone, a strong point to show,
Our strength we know and never let it go.

Home is the place, a territory ,
A blessing from Almighty, which we owe,
A pleasant and a peaceful emotion that flow,
We like it whether fast or slow and never it let go.

Home is the place, a territory,
A feeling of warmth, when it is chilled and snow,
It is tranquility, no matter, through what I go
Your are my soul's home, and I will never let you go.

35. Peaceful Home

I miss you today
Without any reason...
My emotions are changing
With this change in season.

I was smiling yesterday
Bright like sunshine,
My eyes are raining today
It's dark here, but I'm fine.

Yeah it's thundering
And it sounds scary...
I am alone so I'm waiting
For you to come like a fairy

Keep your hand on my head
Tell me to calm down a bit,
Wipe my dried tears
And say it will be alright.

Your smile alone is enough
To make me feel I am safe.

Then no matter how long it rains
I won't ask for escape!

36. I'll cherish you like the leaf

I'll cherish you like the leaf
That I put betwixt pages of my book.
I'll make sure to protect it at all costs
With all the love that I have took.

And after years when it'll be dried
It will still give the warmth in winter.
It will leave a little fragrance
Smelling like love in the summer.

You're the tree that leaf grew on
But you'll be gone one day.
To be resurrected into paper,
Cut down and carried far away.

You will be becoming better
You will always be helpful for sure.
Whenever you'll start growing again
We'll be there, nestling once more.

37. Her Voice !!

She said something is coming up
And we will get to hear her voice.
I can't stop thinking about it
But I have to wait, there's no choice!

Her voice, echoes, yes! It echoes
Like a sea wave, tickling my ears.
So when she mentioned this surprise
Now we can see how everyone stares.

All eyes and ears on her
Because it's something new.
What her voice does to us
Oh! If only she knew...

Everyone is busy counting down
Waiting for the day.
Escape her sweet but rapid breathe?
Try, although there is no way!

38. I see you in my dreams

I see you in my dreams
In cold weather with a cup of tea
In peace, far away from the chaos
It's just you and me

You clicking my pictures
Me capturing you in my eyes
Lying down on ground
Looking up at the skies

You handing me your jacket
To keep the cold breeze away...
With warmth of this love
I wish forever we could stay

Making beautiful memories
With the beauty of this nature
I'll dream about this every night
Although there's no such future

I know we're miles apart
Like a sunflower and the sun

But I wonder what it'd be like
To meet you like this in person...

39. Somewhere You Hide

Somewhere You hide,
Somewhere inside,
Somewhere I used to
Weep, hiding my face,
Somewhere there flows
A broken brook
with crying ripples,
Somewhere I used to lie
Humming a tune
Which You brought in now,
Somewhere Fate will wait
Till You be my Spring.

40. It was all about us

It was me it was you
It was all about us
We danced in the rain
And we looked at the stars,

It was no it was yes
We tangled silk rope
We won and we lost
But we never lost hope,

We ran we sang
We fought and we prayed
We broke a lot of promises
But we never ever betrayed

We read we wrote
We lost and found words
We brought a lot of cages
And then freed the birds,
We walked we stopped
We looked at our eyes
We lived in each other

Knowing how a man dies.

It was all about us :>

41. Mr. Fake

Hey! Mr.fake

Hope so you are doing well and playing again with someone else heart!

I still remember the promises of your fakeness,

That we will stay with each other forever no matter what will happen!

Hey! Mr.fake

Do you still do the same promises to other girls....

That you will be with them forever? Or,

Do you tell them about your kindness and respect towards women,

Which you don't use to do!!!

Hey! Mr.fake Do you still say that you will be the last love of my entire life......

I don't bother about my past, or anything else which sounds more ridiculous!

Hey! Mr.fake Are you still having the enthusiasm to play with someone's feelings???

42. Journey

Honesty is the secret
of happiness
Knowledge is the
path to success
This wisdom I got

from my long journey
Always I am my friend
in this silence Journey
Trying and trying....
Going and going .....
As much as I can
it's the journey of an
unknown boy.

43. Better version of yourself

I wasted so many years in trying to do and be good for everyone.
But did that really went right? No.
So I stared at myself in the mirror and
told myself over and over that I look good,
even though I didn't believe it.
The more I told myself I was good,
the more I began to feel good about myself.
Eventually, it began to return when
I started to truly believe in what I began to represent.
I started to dress the way I wanted to felt,
not the way I wanted to be looked at.
I wanted free flowing clothes that I could move in, not the
clothes pinching me.
I started to writing poem because it made me feel good.
I went for walking daily.
Instead of going out with people,
I went out with myself.
When I spent more time with myself,
I learned what I liked,
I became happier than I had ever been before.

I learned to be true to myself, not someone else.
I realized that I had been incomplete
without the self-knowledge required to define
my own boundaries, my likes, and my dislikes.
And I came to realize this Instead of finding people in your life,
try to find yourself first.
Because the more you will spend time with yourself,
the more you will know that the less you know about yourself.

44. Spread love and positivity.....

The most of the common reasons
for not getting the love that we want,
is we don't Express our feelings
to that person whom we love,
instead we start to expect that person
to understand ourselves without
telling them our feelings.
So just Express your feeling,
but without any expectations.
Spread love and positivity
but without any expectations
of getting the same in return.

45. Move On ?

It's said that, you should always move on,
why would one stop in hell, keep moving,
moving on is rule of life.
But, did anyone teach you how to move on?
How to get out of the hell?
How do deal with the trigger you go through daily?
How to handle that situation ?
How how and how to move on?
Did anyone tell you?
We all heard that ignoring it, not thinking about it,
trying to be happy,
distracting yourself these are the ways to move on.
But my friend is it that easy?
If yes, we all might not search for ways on the internet,
we might not search that relatable content
and talk over how accurate it is.
Indeed moving on is the choice,
but, is it that easy?
Does the trigger stop?
Do you feel happy or relaxed as you felt it before the mess?
Does life get back to normal?
I don't have the answer, do you?

46. Overthinker

Dedicating to all the people who overthink a lot.
Just stop worrying you know no matter
what you do they are always gonna judge you.
So stop wasting time thinking about what would they say?
Did I do it right? Will it be okay?
Stop all the scenarios.
know it's easy to say but hard to do.
All i ask you to do is that it's fine
if you make a mistake so don't doubt yourself,
it's fine to not know about certain things
so don't lose your confidence.
Just go with flow and stop thinking.
Embrace the day and don't ruminate.

47. Busy World

Sometimes you just want to take a pause
and be in the moment!
Always rushing, never enough time,
having too much to do is our reality. Right ?
We sometimes feel that our schedule controls us
and because we are smart, caring and committed people,
we can always add just one more thing.
Even now when many of us are studying at home or school,
we feel we have little time,
and we continue to rush.
It has become so much a part of our lives that
we never ask ourselves why we are rushing.
By letting go of rushing
we become friends with now and learn
to bring our best selves to the present moment.

48. A Mother's love

When I was young I outgrew shoes
that made me a little faster, a little taller.
Outgrew my jacket with fur lined pockets
which kept small hands a little warmer.
Outgrew favourite games I played.
Outgrew my first bike, my first bed.
Outgrew my first teenage crush,
my first heartbreak, and a few old friends.
But no matter how old I get
on the days when I'm not enough,
when I need to do better, stand a little taller,
when nothing can warm me up,
she's there, she's always there
knowing me better than anyone does.
I'll never outgrow her, only grow to know her,
and all the ways that a mother loves.

49. Sleepless Nights

I cried for several nights,
wondering where it all went wrong
What did I do to deserve this much suffering?
I had my heart crushed like it was some toy.
Those sleepless nights, those nights where
I could physically feel the pain in my heart
Where I just wanted it to stop and vanish in some way
Thinking about those all nights still gives me chills.
The heartbreak was almost unbearable to survive.
It almost took everything in me
The possibility of loving again
The possibility of trusting again,
The desire to knock on the door of love and walk the journey of
heartbreak again.

50. Destination

I often dream of being on the road
without an end in sight,
no destination to reach and
yet a journey that feels like destination itself,
where the meaning of destination
continues to change by every passing day,
until one day I truly realise
that we were never after a destination all this time,
but in search of a journey
where we continue to find
ourselves at every passing moment,
Where we continue to arrive at
the only destination that matters, ourselves.